CONFESSIONS OF A HOOLIGAN

Sergei Esenin is the most popular Russian poet of this century. Born in 1895 into the Russian peasantry, he went to Moscow as a youth, where he welcomed the 1917 Revolution as the herald of a Peasant Utopia. Later, he grew disillusioned with the Bolshevik industrialising policy. His poetic life became a muted, pathetic outcry against the destruction of the archetypal 'wooden Russia' of his childhood and imagination. In 1922 he married Isadora Duncan—a brief liaison. In 1925 he married a grand-daughter of Tolstoy. Later in the year he suffered a nervous breakdown and, in December, he slit his wrists and hanged himself in a hotel room, having written his last poem in his own blood. He left one of the most formidable poetic achievements in Russian literature, a poetry of remarkable intensity and clarity.

Geoffrey Thurley, in this first extensive collection of Esenin's poetry to be published in English, introduces the poet in his social and literary context and describes his language and forms. Mr Thurley is a teacher at the University of Adelaide, Australia; he is a poet and critic as well as a translator.

TRANSLATIONS

General Editors: Daniel Weissbort and Michael Schmidt

Guillaume Apollinaire *Hunting Horns* by Barry Morse
Paul Celan *Nineteen Poems* by Michael Hamburger
Natalya Gorbanevskaya *Poems, The Trial, Prison* by Daniel Weissbort
Nazim Hikmet *The Day Before Tomorrow* by Taner Baybars
Vladimir Mayakovsky *Wi the Haill Voice* by Edwin Morgan
Dan Pagis *Selected Poems* by Stephen Mitchell
Fernando Pessoa *I-IV* by Jonathan Griffin
Provençal Poems by Sally Purcell
East German Poetry, a dual-language anthology by Michael Hamburger

forthcoming

Tristan Corbière *Wreckes* by Val Warner (dual language)
Mahmoud Darwish *Selected Poems* by Ian Wedde
Attila József *Selected Poems and Texts* by John Batki, George Gömöri and
James Atlas
Kyozo Takagi *Poems* by James Kirkup
Alexander Tvardovsky *Selected Writings* by C. P. Snow
and Anthony Rudolf

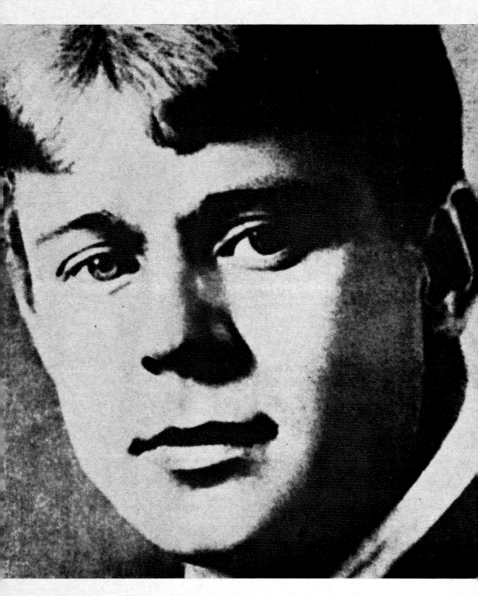

Sergei Esenin

CONFESSIONS OF A HOOLIGAN

fifty poems by

Sergei Esenin

translated from the Russian and introduced by

Geoffrey Thurley

TRANSLATIONS
A CARCANET PRESS PUBLICATION

Copyright © Geoffrey Thurley 1973

SBN 902145 48 7—cloth
SBN 85635 001 X—paper

All Rights Reserved

First published 1973
by Carcanet Press Limited
266 Councillor Lane
Cheadle Hulme, Cheadle
Cheshire SK8 5PN

Acknowledgements are due to *Modern Poetry in Translation*
where some of these translations first appeared.

Note:
Titles of the poems are either the first line of the poem or Esenin's own title, except
where marked with an asterisk on the contents pages, in which case the title has been
supplied by the translator.

Printed in Great Britain
by W & J Mackay Limited, Chatham

CONTENTS

INTRODUCTION

NOWHERE is the gulf between 'culture' and 'reality' more embarrassing than in the context of the Russian Revolution and the Great War. Much as the War wrenched the Keatsian sensibility of Wilfred Owen into premature sagacity, so the Revolution, first by its awful menace, then by its much more awful actuality, shocked a generation of Russian intellectuals from play into politics. Every Russian poet alive and writing at that time was political, whether his reaction to events were exile, silence, acclamation or despair. This is not to say that all reactions were equal, or to deny that some were more useful than others. One should have been grateful not to have been confronted by the situation in the first place; but one should also recognize the fact that Russia shipped abroad much of its least valuable merchandise in the years after the Revolution. Writers like Bunin, Remizov and Rozanov and the emigré musicians who flocked around Diaghilev, represented the slighter more graceful side of the Russian cultural personality, a side that is easily overlooked, much as Borodin is overshadowed by Tchaikovsky and Turgenev by Dostoyevsky. By and large those that stayed and endured—Pasternak, Mayakovsky, Blok—produced the work that mattered, even if they were destroyed in the process. The four major poets of the period—Blok, Esenin, Mayakovsky and Pasternak—outsurvived each other, to perish at oddly regular intervals, like the four finishers in a relay-race: Blok lasted only four years after the Revolution, Esenin another four after that; Mayakovsky another five; then, breaking the symmetry, Pasternak, who ought by right to have perished in the 1937 purges, proved the most resilient of them all, and saw the thing through. Pasternak's survival itself is a tremendous tribute to the man of greatness. (Why, after all, *was* he allowed to survive?) But the production of *Dr. Zhivago* late in life was consistent with the rule established by Blok in *The Twelve* and Esenin in *Soviet Russia*: the suffering that poets have always traditionally hankered after swats out the little men like flies, and reveals the truly great for what they are—men who face whatever happens, and offer themselves as experimental subjects. The reader must forgive me if this sounds like another plea for suffering. One is personally only too grateful to have been spared the horrors these men lived through; all men of sense and good will seek to avoid suffering, and only a charlatan pretends

7

to worship it. But precisely because of this, we should praise the strength and courage of great poets, not only in its human capacity—poets suffer no more than other men, and other men are just as brave—but for the evidence they afford us of a more valuable function poetry can perform than we usually allow for. It was enough to survive the Revolution and the Civil War and the purges: to do what Esenin does in 'Mare Ships' (p. 37) and Blok in *The Twelve*, Pasternak in *Zhivago*, Mayakovsky in his later poetry —this seems simply implausible, until we see in it only an extreme form of the poetic process. To retain not only awareness and sympathy, but also a pitiless conception of the self and its history, this is the function of poetry under duress, and this is what we see so triumphant in the work of the great Russian poets of this century.

The facts of Esenin's life can be derived from the poems, which form, as they do not, say, in the case of Alexander Blok or Dylan Thomas, a continuous and frank autobiography of the sensibility. By this I mean that the state of mind experienced and the stages of awareness reached by the poet do not have to be inferred or translated out of mandarin symbolism, but are hawked and proffered by a man who never—thank God!—outgrew a certain peasant crudeness and emotionalism. The material of his declamatory confessional verse comes from three sources—his childhood in Ryazan, the Revolution, and the poet's own debaucheries. Esenin was thirty years old when he hanged himself: for the last six or seven of these years he had been occupied with making himself the greatest exhibition in Russian life. He had become helplessly alcoholic, and was continually in and out of prisons and sanatoriums. The Isadora Duncan farce, the rowdy trips abroad, the ambivalence towards Communism—all these things expressed the same inward confusion. Esenin's final act of suicide—by hanging himself in a hotel room—only completed a process of self-immolation that had started, so he confessed in the verse letter to his wife, out of fear and horror before the facts of Revolution:

> I live in thick smoke,
> And the shattering blast of things
> That torture me because I do not understand
> Where this century is leading us.

Even granting a degree of self-justification here as elsewhere in the longer apologetic poems of the 'twenties—Esenin lacked the intellectual sophistication to probe very subtly into himself—we cannot help admiring the courage and fundamental honesty of Esenin's reponse to what his life had become. If we turn from him to any Western poet who might offer parallel

8

with him—say Hart Crane or Dylan Thomas—we cannot, I think, refrain from granting to the Russian poet a superior openness and frankness. In fact, Esenin's very absence of introspection aids him in this. Dylan Thomas's verse, for instance, offers practically no evidence of the shoddy disorder of so much of his later life; Hart Crane acknowledged the falling apart of body and soul under the stress of violent debauch with a fullness that at times attains sublimity: there is nothing in Esenin, I think, to equal the majestic transmutation of material we see in Crane's 'Island Quarry' or 'North Labrador'. But Crane's very sublimity contains an element of fraud: the conception of poetry implicit in Esenin's much more human ordinariness is surely saner and sounder than Crane's consistent concentration on what the imagination spans 'beyond despair'. The formula expressed in that famous phrase from 'For the Marriage of Faustus and Helen' itself suggests the self-defeating unreality of Crane's whole adventure, although this unreality became a constituent of the pathos of his greatest work.

Esenin's work spans only fifteen years. It begins with a simplicity that shames the premature nobility of the early Blok. Lyrics like 'Night' (p. 26), and 'Already Evening' (p. 25) owe something perhaps to the indirect influence of Goethe, but Esenin's pristine clarity is his own. Like other writers of working-class stock—one thinks of D. H. Lawrence and Maxim Gorky —Esenin was a child in his childhood, unlike Proust, for instance, or Yeats or Rilke, bourgeois poets who seem to have been born middle-aged. Markov and Sparks' dismissal of the very early work as 'extremely unoriginal and inept'[1] must certainly be rejected. Esenin had enjoyed the incomparable privileges of an under-privileged Childhood, of a childhood, that is to say, without any of the cultural interference that made a horrible little adult of Proust's Marcel. 'The Birch Tree' of 1914 (p. 27), is a perfect and exquisite piece, miraculously unconscious of its own simplicity, yet sure in diction and movement. (The poem appeared in the collection called *Zaryanka—Poems for Children*; the finest pieces in this set stand among the best poems ever written for children, genuinely artless and devoid of condescension.)

Still, there is no denying the greater interest of the poems Esenin began to produce under the shadow of the Revolution. Esenin's greatest gift perhaps is a certain peasant fullness of gaze which was never quite allowed to cloud over. The peasant is far from the Arcadian stereotype, of course: he is crafty and hard as well as simple, and his very naïveté is cunning, compact of hidden knowledge and the residue of ancient cults. He is also incurably superstitious: scratch any Russian, indeed, and you get not a Tartar (that is a White Russian romanticism) but a hopeless, medieval

[1] V. Markov and M. Sparks, *Modern Russian Poetry*, London, 1966, p. 838.

Believer. It is a combination of all these qualities that gives Esenin's pre-Revolutionary lyrics their special beauty. Blok was the last poet of the sublime in Russia, and we shall look in vain through Esenin's work for the exalted majesty of a poem like 'Spring' ('At the crossroads Where distance begins'); moreover, Blok subsumes traditional Christian orthodoxy under a Goethean calm, if never quite a Wordsworthian depth:

> And the crosses—and the distant panes—
> And the tops of the jagged forest—
> Everything breathes with the lazy
> White measure
> Of Spring.

Poetry like this proves that Nature doesn't belong to the peasant, and it is not Esenin's intimate knowledge of Nature's wrinkles and seams that makes his lyrics often more breathtaking than Blok's religiose and philosophical offerings. Precisely the greater spiritual breadth and cultural awareness of Blok's work deny it the devastating, simple sophistication of Esenin's Christian symbolism. Take this poem, 'Easter' (p. 29):

> Last year's leaves litter the ravine
> Beneath the shrubs, a copper mass;
> And a man in a smock of sunshine
> Rides by on the russet ass.
>
> Softer than flax is His hair,
> But clouded his face and manner.
> The fir-trees bow before him there,
> And greet Him with *Hosanna!*

I must apologize if my translation here reads a little like the Methodist hymnal. Unconsciously, I had striven to reproduce an English equivalent of Esenin's simple yet relaxed piety. For there was no equivalent in Russian life to the widespread cultural and spiritual influence of the nonconformist church movements in nineteenth-century England and America. Thus, for the Russian, no matter what his background, Christianity meant the massive, stultified grandeur of the Orthodox Church, clanging harmonies on great bells, onion-domed temples, subterranean bass intonations, and the lavish prostration of the believer. There could be no equivalent in Russian literature, therefore, to the quizzical intimacy that is so attractive in Emily Dickinson and D. H. Lawrence, just as there was no equivalent in Russian working-class life to the independent thinking and worship of the Black Country artisans, with their long tradition of free communion with a God who descended into their grimy brick temples. The socio-political and the religious histories are inextricably intertwined. The Western reader coming to poets like Esenin must prepare himself for an absolute prostration of the self before the authority of a medieval God. What my translation of Esenin's 'Easter' reflects, therefore, (in so far as it reflects anything) is not the metrical quaintness of low-church hymnody, but the release through the quasi-ballad metre of Pushkin of a simple yet powerful Christian emotion. The clear, emphatic Christian symbols and personifications of the poems of these years provide some of the richest effects in Esenin's work. The man in the 'smock of sunshine', the sparrow reading from his Psaltery in the forest, the red calf of the sunset, the red prayer-book of dawn, St. Andrew piping among the willows, Isaiah tending the golden herds—these symbols and personifications leap from the page with the freshness of great, primal poetry: Esenin interprets the facts of Nature through the symbolic filters of Christian and pagan myth, yet with no loss of directness and naïveté. (There is a parallel of sorts in the primal symbolism of some of Swinburne's work and Francis Thompson's, though the effect in their verse is often obscured by literary sophistica-tion.) Esenin's personifications come from a primitive layer of the mind, yet they are at the service of a subtle linguistic sense. The syndrome is typically Russian: between the sublime and the primitive there is little intermediate thought. Hence the peculiar quality of so much Russian art—its tendency towards hysteria, its irascible cunning simplicity. Russia has yet to produce a real philosopher, and its 'civilization' hardly exists.

This pristine early phase of Esenin's career culminates in the series of brilliant poems and sequences in which he acclaimed the Revolution. The Revolution cauterized Blok into *The Twelve*, then left him for dead, a worn-out shell. Esenin was a generation younger—twenty-two at the outbreak of Revolution, as opposed to Blok's thirty-seven—and of peasant, not high bourgeois stock. He greeted the Revolution with 'Otherwhere', 'The Dove of Jordan' (p. 36) and 'Requiem', among others—poems which translate the political events into ecstatically mystical terms. The verse is limpid, ravishingly fresh, sparkling—

> My golden earth! You bright
> Cathedral of Autumn!

Esenin is not only unashamed of his Christianity (though he later confessed that he had been)—he insists on interpreting the political apocalypse in overtly Biblical terms:

> And there Saint Andrew plays
> His flute among the pollards.

> On the edge of the village
> A maiden-mother, sick
> And angry with Knowledge,
> Beats an ass with a stick.

Esenin's flat countryside had always been interpenetrated with religious mythology. Now it appears as a 'rustic Jordan land', and the Easter dove heralds the Revolution as the baptism of the new age:

> And here is the dove, borne
> Aloft in the wind's hand.
> It smokes with a new dawn,
> My rustic Jordan land.

Esenin's poetry at this stage is intensely exhilarating, vibrant with the idea of the realized Utopia. The contrast with Blok's hag-ridden masterpiece—a deliberate act of self-abuse—could hardly be greater.

Soviet criticism, which was for a long time silent about Esenin, has learned to take this kind of religiosity in its stride—with a little help from Esenin himself: 'I would ask the reader to regard all my Jesuses and Mothers of God and Archangel Michaels,' he wrote in the Preface to the 1924 collection of his works, 'as so much poetic fable. I can no more deny this phase by expunging it from myself, than humanity itself can wipe out a period of 2000 years of Christian culture, but all these liturgical proper names must be taken as names representative of certain myths—Osiris, St. John, Zeus, Aphrodite, Athene, etc.' M. T. Yumin, in a sensitive though to Western eyes lop-sided account of Esenin's poetry,[1] rightly notes here the continuity of Esenin's methodology: 'All these images,' he writes, having immediately above cited a dozen instances, from Esenin's so-called 'October' poems, 'are constructed according to the principle already familiar to us of the comparison of disparate phenomena so characteristic of the earlier Esenin.' This formulation would not have surprised Coleridge; it is difficult to think of any other way of making poetic imagery work. But Yumin has grasped the essential mainspring of Esenin's art—the bold yet often subtle collocation of image. The techniques derive substantially from Symbolism, in spite of the so-called revolt of many young Russian poets of Esenin's time against the elder statesmen, Blok and Byely. Renato Poggioli, by contrast, throws in the towel, and gives in to vague metaphysics. He describes Esenin's lyrics as being 'devoid of any rhetorical and anecdotal structure, and lightly woven on a cobweb of transparent words around the cluster of a few bright and startling images.'[2] No poetry

---

[1] P. F. Yumin: *Sergei Esenin*, Moscow 1969.
[2] R. Poggioli, The Poets of Russia, Harvard, 1960, p. 273.

was ever made like this, least of all Esenin's. It would be a simple matter to demonstrate that Esenin's lyrics are put together solidly and simply, on a basis of sustained situational points of view. In other words, they follow the principle of Romantic verse in 'taking place'—in a field, on a highroad, in a hotel room. The structure is guaranteed both by the integrity of the situation and locale and by the poet's tone of voice: Esenin uses the analogical techniques of Symbolism, but the tone of his verse is insistently personal and inflected, like that of Byron and Lermontov. Yumin is right to follow through the consistent analogical procedures of the earliest pieces for children (e.g., the pine in 'First Snow' like 'a white handkerchief') to the 'October' poems, which transpose the traditional Christian symbols to a new philosophical level, so that Russia is likened to Jordan, for instance, and the Revolution to Christ's baptism. 'In the poems on other themes,' Yumin writes,[1] 'the earlier Esenin methods continue to be heard, and the manner of poetic incarnation peculiar to him is preserved.' Far from there being any break in his development, the movement of his early verse converges upon the Revolution, funnels through it, so that the bright, simple, yet age-old Christian beliefs are simply lifted to a new sociophilosophical level of application.

But between these poems of 1918, acclaiming the Revolution, and those even of the following year, there is a terrible gulf. In 1919, in quatrains markedly close in style to those of 'The Dove of Jordan', Esenin wrote 'Mare Ships'. The intensity of this poem—an intensity bordering upon derangement—betrays the sheer strain that had underlain the exultations of the 'Dove': in place of its apocalyptic fervour, with its brimming religious light and its transfigured fields, 'Mare Ships' is compact of bitter disgust, the disgust of physical filth, decay, hunger, wretchedness:

> Not rye, but frost leaps the field.
> Smashed windows, gaping doors.
> Even the sun-light freezes
> Like a gelding's stale piss.

The Revolution has happened; Esenin's bluff has been called. He ridicules the Pentecostal blisses of the 'Dove':

> I sang the wondrous guest, it's clear,
> In self-derision.

Esenin's taste for fine clothes, exotic women, cosmopolitan high life and expensive debauch found itself offended by the immediate effects of the Revolution, much as, we may be sure, it would have been by the greyness of Soviet life after Stalin. Rather to his surprise, the poet discovers within

[1] op. cit. p. 213.

13

himself an Olympianism which had in fact been patronizing the workers. Once again, the miracle is that the poet has been able to keep his head, at the expense, perhaps, of the man. Esenin's quatrains have a new poise here, a new maturity of judgement, which results in an epigrammatic wit recalling Horace and Marvell:

> If the wolf bays a star
> Cloud has consumed the sky.
> Ripped-open bowels of mares.
> And the crows' black sails glide by.

From 1919 to 1921, Esenin was associated with Imaginism, a movement purportedly derived from Imagism, but in fact futurist-symbolist, if not actually decadent. It spoke of the poetic image as 'naphthalene which preserves the work of art from the moths of time'. It also exploited the fashionable talk about the Image (*obraz* in Russian) as opposed to Symbol (*simvol*) in order to emphasize the hermeticism of the poetic venture much in the spirit of Mallarmé, if not Gautier. The theoretic doctrines put forward in the *Deklaratsia* of 1921, signed by Esenin, are not original or very clear. What is interesting is the aggressiveness of its reaction against the Soviet regime and the idea of the Revolution: for the poet all politics is bourgeois, and a socialist revolution is as much a betrayal of the essence of the human spirit as a tyrannical monarchy. Soviet critics have stressed Esenin's ignorance of the real aims of the Revolution. He was, like Blok, happy to acclaim the millenium and to rejoice in the transfiguration of souls; but when the mystic transfiguration failed to take place, and the new state had to get on with the business of administration, he lost interest and felt betrayed, in true bourgeois fashion. But on their own level, the poets understood very well what had happened—too well for Soviet critics. Blok's *The Twelve* and Esenin's 'Mare Ships' don't tell us much about the economics of Revolution, but they tell us a lot about the human mind's more basic needs. Nothing, to be sure, is more basic than the need to eat and work. But when the food is procured and the fed are in work, the questions raised by the poets must be faced, by the Soviet government as much as by any other.

The next phase of Esenin's creative life begins with the first of the 'Hooligan' poems. 'The Confession' itself (p. 45) was written in 1918, though not published until 1920. More correctly, the phase begins with the altered mental processes that prompted the self-destructive turn his life now irrevocably took. Yumin notes the development in the Imaginist poems of two dominant themes—'the cold, at times hostile attitude towards the new order, and the unsatisfactoriness of his own fate.'[1] It is true

[1] op. cit. p. 246.

that there was a good deal of bourgeois bohemianism in Imaginism (they saw themselves as Apaches), and that some of the flagrant coarseness in Esenin's poems of this period (women are 'otters', and 'arses'—*zadnitsa*—and thighs—*lyazki*—abound) reflects the unintelligent influence of Mariengof and Shershenevitch. But Yumin is certainly wrong to diagnose here a general decline in Esenin's work. The brutalism and coarseness, like the grotesque imagery ('women hatch a third Eye slowly from the womb'), reflect the deep disruption in Esenin's mind caused by the Revolution. Like Blok, Esenin had had the courage and the intelligence not to flinch at the vital moment, which means not simply that he put on a show of maintaining his pre-Revolutionary enthusiasm, but that at the layers of the mind where poetry is forged he kept faith with his pretensions. But the Revolution did appalling violence to what he most admired and loved in life. The importance of the act of recollection in the creation of poetry makes poets basically conservative creatures. Esenin was revolted more deeply than he could ever have dreamed possible not only by the carnage and squalor—so much worse than the time-honoured almost Biblical poverty of the past—but by the inevitable industrialization to which, it was obvious, the Revolution was but the dissonant prelude. Many of the most moving poems of this period turn on the mechanization of the countryside he loved so much. In poems like 'I am the last poet of the village' (1920, p. 42), Esenin deplores the horrible depredations of technology. The new roads strangle the villages, and the animal servants of the old life attempt vainly to compete with the 'iron guest' of the new order. At the same time, a new note begins to dominate the poet's thinking about himself—he had been drinking hard for several years, and in the early 'twenties was working strenuously to establish the evil reputation he spent so much time lamenting. It is interesting how with him being a roaring boy becomes a vocation of a slightly more professional kind than we see in Dylan Thomas. Thomas's rowdiness was an accepted embarrassment, a time-honoured pastime that helped him to identify himself as a 'poet'. Esenin's was a profession: he became a '*skandalist*' much as Wallace Stevens became a company director. At the same time, his scandalism betokened something more than exhibitionist irresponsibility: it was a way of expressing sympathy—of the profoundest kind—with the animals and natural organisms he saw being destroyed by the new age. He too was being strangled by progress:

> Just as in a concrete jacket
> Man has padlocked Nature
>
> So the wild fire dies within me
> Dictated by the self-same laws.

Regret for the past, despair at what he was doing to himself, become the key modes of his last five years' writing. Poem after poem turns upon his evil reputation, his exhaustion, his hangovers, his sense of his own brutalism. This is how Mikhail Zoshchenko saw Esenin in 1921: 'A man comes to our table, walking uncertainly. He is wearing a black velvet blouse. There is a large white muslin bow on his chest. His face is smeared with powder. His lips are made up and his eyes pencilled. On his face is a smile —a drunken and rather embarrassed smile. Someone says: "Seryozha, come and sit with us." Now I see it is Esenin.'

The photographs reveal a peasant—broad, coarse good looks, an attractive recklessness, slightly flashy clothes. And there is a tone of brutal recklessness about the poems of this time, accompanied often by a self-pitying lacrimosity. Yet the impressive thing really is that he does not ever quite do a Marmeladov; he does not, that is, degenerate into the whining self-flagellation characteristic of so much Russian writing. His confessions are on the whole frank, occasionally bolstered by a possibly suspect rationale:

> I only played the hooligan
> To burn with an intenser flame.

This puts Esenin a little too glibly into the Rimbaud *poète maudit* tradition, and this is a pity, because his rowdyness and the bitter fruits it bore are chronicled with a realistic wit and an uncanny objectivity that stand out against the decadent futility of so much Western poetry of the time. More authentic is the simple registering of the facts themselves, sometimes with amusement, more often with a dawning horror, more often still with a phlegmatic detachment that may be his greatest gift:

> I'm tired of this pointless pain;
> A strange smile on my face
> I love to bear in a light frame,
> The calm light and the dead man's peace.

This surely is the 'terrifying clairvoyance' Eliot praised in Shakespeare. Esenin's great quality is often held to be his lyricism, his gift of 'song', which challenges comparison, so we are told, with that of Pushkin. Yet although this view can't be dismissed out of hand, it certainly represents a distorting simplification of the truth. For one thing, the memory of Pushkin is often a curse to Esenin. One tires of the easy trick of the metre, the plangent though often casual rhymes, the almost invariable quatrains, the couplets brought back again with a crashingly 'moving' impact, the battery of the effects Russian poets still find it so hard to resist for long— flying cranes, nightingales, snowstorms, troikas, sleigh-bells etc. Often it is hard for a Western reader to believe that this verse was being written at the same time that Pound was writing the *Cantos*, Eliot *The Waste Land*, Lawrence *Birds, Beasts and Flowers*, Apollinaire his *Calligrammes*. The metres are often metronomically tied to their text-book models, and everything is sacrificed to the emotive impact of the rhyme. At about this time, of course, Russian poetry was not standing still: Mayakovsky's 'A Cloud in Trousers' which effectively breaks with every prosodic model, was written in 1914. Marina Tsvetayeva and Anna Akhmatova, moreover, had started exploring the possibilities of a much more private, hesitant poetry which necessitated new rhythms, closer perhaps to those of the Pound of *Lustra*. So Esenin was something of a dinosaur—a peasant, with the small-town hick's ambitions to be a new Pushkin. Thus, he restored, or rather tried to maintain in currency, the emotion-soaked balladry Pushkin had purveyed so incomparably. Even so, it seems fair to say that Russian poets even today find it hard altogether to surmount the conception of poetry as a declaimed, threnodic art, which smashes the listener over the head, and exploits shamelessly the resources of the cruder sonic devices of verse. Russian poetry consistently falls foul of its own rhythmic persistency: rhythm takes charge of imagery, tone and structure, so that the poem's 'real' inner content sometimes seems sacrificed to the residual content of the Romantic formal procedures. Russian poetry to some extent parallels English in its powerful rhythms: yet there is much less in Russian poetry of what Hopkins called 'counterpointed rhythm'; that is, the metric pattern is less often and less subtly played off against a different superimposed rhythm. Rhythm, in other words, seems often to be synonymous with metre. These very general observations, which I am conscious are contradicted by numerous examples, seem to me nonetheless to help us in focusing the precise nature of Esenin's strengths—and weaknesses.

The poems Esenin wrote in the 'twenties fall into two main groups: first, heightened, tautened versions of the lyric quatrain; second, almost-free-verse conversational narratives, anecdotal, confessional and even ideological. It is presumably this latter group of which Pasternak so stringently disapproved,[1] and presumably it is the sometimes orthodox Communist content as well as the apparently slovenly versification which made Pasternak shudder. Yet although there are certainly signs of fatigue hereabouts, signs that Esenin could no longer sustain the weight of the formal lyric as easily as he had earlier, the success of longer poems such as 'Soviet Russia' (p. 68) and 'My Path' (p. 97), and the various verse letters he wrote to his relations, proves that Esenin knew what he was up to. The lyric quatrain is useful for expressing crystallized situations and symbols; for narrative, it is practically useless. Thus when, later in life, he cast his mind

---

[1] See his Essay in *Autobiography*, translated by Manya Harari, London, 1968.

back over his career, he used a freer, more dilatory rhythm, only loosely bound together with rhyme, which allowed him to reflect, to discuss, to describe and to narrate without awkward transition. It is an impressive achievement, and the finest of these poems—'Soviet Russia' and 'The Black Man' (p. 102)—are among his best work. The other group, the quatrain lyrics, have a different purpose. It is in these poems—'The Rowan Tree Fire' (p. 77), 'I will not weep' (p. 49), 'This present sadness is not eased' (p. 61), 'Now little by little we depart' (p. 78)—that Esenin distils himself most clearly: these poems achieve at times a classical purity of movement that fully justifies the Pushkin-like manner. They are an important part of the small body of great twentieth century poetry: the classical structure and tone are not superadded, but derive from a full assimilation of refractory experience never rejected, even when most regretted. Esenin's repeated assurance that he regrets nothing must, I think, be accepted in all good faith. It is neither Stoic attitudinizing nor stubbornness; on the contrary, no one ever acknowledged his mistakes more wisely ('Little of what has passed is dear, And many the errors made'). It is rather a refusal to disown himself or to disclaim responsibility for what he has done and become. It is an admission that even ones mistakes—especially ones mistakes, perhaps—are part of oneself, and that it was better to have lived recklessly, even brutally, than never to have lived at all. The recklessness of a brave man is worth more than the caution of a coward, even when that caution is justified by events—perhaps because inaction can never be justified positively, and justification is only negative.

Esenin's is a lonely poetry. It rarely admits others into its world. He accuses a woman of coldness, he begs her for animal communion *faute de mieux*; there is an obscure man-love ('Would that his head like a golden rose Beckoned me onward through the lilac Smoke'), and the suicide note is addressed to a male friend. But the essential situation in Esenin, as in Hart Crane, is one of solitude, the solitude of the poet in the 'golden grove' in what is perhaps his greatest lyric ('The Rowan Tree Fire'); or the much more horrible solitude of the alcoholic, in 'The Black Man', and the various poems written in sanatoriums and jails. Esenin paid the usual price for hoarding a great gift and making it the price of his acceptance by other men—sterile isolation and despair. As he hardened in his despair, as the release of alcohol became more and more enclosing, so his isolation became the more unbreachable. But perhaps only a very isolated man is forced into a genuinely political relation with other men: it was precisely Esenin's refusal to stop analysing and dramatizing his own 'greatness' that opened up for him the nature of society itself. For this sort of reason, I think 'Soviet Russia' has claims to being his greatest single poem. It preserves the classical sweep of his finest lyrics—

That storm has passed. And few of us survive—

—along with the reflective, flexible discursiveness that allows him to register the complex facts of the social revolution he is witnessing. The poem is *about* a Sovietized Russia, but it *is* Esenin's rather pitiable situation within it. It offers a brutal and accurate picture of the political realities— the clumsy peasants trying to wrap away minds stiffened by centuries of the subservience that to Western ears is somehow suggested in the very sound of the Russian word for Orthodox—*pravoslavny*—; the harsh Young Communists whooping agit-prop doggerel into the night; the deep groans of the *babas*, registering the utter bewilderment of the older people. At the same time, it realizes the alienation of the poet himself, his sense of being out of the whole thing, yet of having willed it to happen, and therefore of being responsible for it. In this, Esenin provides, I think, a model for the relations between any poet and the rest of human society: the poet is inherently treacherous, continually exhorting the masses to violence and sweeping change, then going back upon his word when anything happens, because deep down he resists being one of *them*. Esenin's political views, like his alcoholism and his kinship with the whores and thugs of the Moscow taverns, only emphasized his aloneness. This aloneness seems more convincing than the good-hearted but ultimately abject attempts, described in 'Stanzas' (p. 65) and 'Return to my Homeland', (p. 74) to get to grips with Marx and Engels. There is something sad about a great spirit grubbing among the worms.

No poem dramatizes this aloneness more devastatingly than 'The Black Man', which takes the form of an address to a character who turns out in the end to be Esenin himself, reflected in the mirror. Esenin had been horribly lucid about his condition in many of his earlier lyrics: he had seen himself as a 'yellow skeleton', and a heap of 'damp and yellow dust'. In a truly terrifying image, he saw himself as being devoured by his own eyes, 'as a maggot chews a blue petal'. As always, Esenin finds his imagery in the commonplace objects of his own life and memory. In 'The Black Man', he extends the image of the plain of snow, which many Russian writers— one thinks of Pushkin and Gogol—had used with powerful symbolic effect, forcing it to yield a new dimension of meaning: the whole plain, he observes, is 'covered In a soft quick-lime'. Thus, a bare month before he wrote his last words in his own blood, he saw deep into his own dissolution.

A note on the translations. A great deal of translation from Russian is being carried out today. The setting up of the Joint Service School for Linguistics in the fifties was certainly a significant cultural factor in

British life. The Slavonic Department Bulge stems directly from it. Regrettably, there seems less cause for jubilation than perhaps there should be. There are several theories of translation current today which seem to me simply heretical. There is Robert Lowell's approach, which enables the translator to run the original through the mangle of his own literary machinery, so that everything, from Catullus to Baudelaire, is reduced to the same process. The idea—which originated perhaps with Pound and his Propertius —is that the poet produces a different *thing*, comparison with the original being odious. But this is absurd, for the imitation isn't a new thing—it has taken over too much material for that. The result must be an adulterous *mélange*, satisfying neither purist nor poet. Like Kurosawa's Shakespeare, Lowell's Baudelaire and Racine are garbled monsters, exercises in style necessarily lacking the tension that holds together the best of Lowell's own poems, yet desecrating the limpid medium through which French thought is transmitted. The idea of the imitation or *version*, then, is an evasion of the rather daunting responsibility of the translator, which really has to be to attempt as complete a 'faithfulness' to the original as is consistent with linguistic sense.

Another contemporary heresy, diametrically opposite to this, yet equally misguided, is that of the so-called literal version. By far the greater number of modern translators adhere to this non-school. The result is the dribble of inert phrases that fills most volumes of modern poetry translation. Complete literalness—as far as this is feasible—must produce a rhythmless sprawl of imagery. The more the poetry in question depends upon imagery, the more plausible this approach will appear. But no poetry, not even H.D.'s or Robert Creeley's or Takahashi's is *just* image. The rhythm of placing and spacing, and the subtler rhythm of consonance and dissonance are enmeshed too exquisitely for any 'purely' visual image pattern to be reproduced. The translator's task is really just as unrewarding and arduous with a Japanese Haiku poet as with a Russian Acmeist or with Vondel or with Goethe. It is easy to feel (however furtively) that a free verse poem is easier to translate than a highly wrought poem with a complex stanza, rhyme and metre pattern. But this is indeed a fallacy. The reverse is true. To persuade oneself—to say nothing of a reader—that a dribble of phrases calls up the poetic response is far more difficult when the original offers no apparent metric precedent than when it intimidates with a battery of rhetorical devices. To grasp the music, the cool powerful structure of a poet like Tadeusz Rozewicz, for example, is more difficult than to sense through the medium of a language that is not ones own the stride and orchestration of a Blok or a Valéry.

Translation is always at best a Pyrrhic victory. The original is as likely to suffer under a translator's attempts to pacify it into rhyme or rhythm schemes that are really alien to it as under another translator's indifference to its musical properties. The translator is a foster-parent, and the child either wilts under the new guardian's indifference or perishes under his rigorousness. Yet some foster parents are as good as natural parents. Here the analogy breaks down: it is rare that a translator will do better than the original poet, though quite possibly he is of superior stature. What of Stefan George's translations of Giraud's *Pierrot Lunaire*, for instance, or Baudelaire's versions of Poe? Anyway, the relationship can be a good one and the sacrifice and suffering occasionally seem worth it. It depends on the qualities of the translator. The *ideal* translator is probably a good poet, but not too good—a poet, in other words, who fulfils himself in realizing another poet's thought in another poet's terms rather than in conceiving and developing his own. Of the alternatives, the translator who isn't a poet at all, or not a very good one, simply won't be able to energise his own language sufficiently; while the very good poet will never quite be able to give the original work everything he has got. There will always be the holding back, the inward reservation. A possible compromise is another modern heresy—that of the tandem translation. Here the front rider knows the language—he was, say, a graduate of the Army Russian Course—while the back pedaller is the poet. This is certainly the worst of all possible approaches to translation. The gap between the poet's and the translator's experience and language is great enough anyway. To add a second gap, between translator and versifier, is much more than to double the initial difficulties: it is to foster a monster, a Frankenstein made up of masticated bits of original poet, literal translator, and second poet.

The inadequacies of these present translations of Esenin will not be more obvious to an intelligent reader who knows Russian and loves poetry than they are to the translator. Sometimes the original has demanded a rhyme-scheme in English for the imagery and thought to make sense. Although a rhyme in Russian can never, obviously, be the same as a rhyme in English, still the effect of a rhymed English cadence does sometimes seem more an equivalent to the original Russian cadence than a purely 'literal' version could supply. Whether the rhyme exists in the translator's own tongue depends on chance, of course: every good translator knows the miraculous joy of a rhyme being offered to him unexpectedly.

Sometimes, on the other hand, the effect depends on a particular collocation of imagery, or on a tone which too vigorous treatment from the translator simply destroys. The act of translation involves as much avoidance as anything else: the translator must avoid both the Scylla of archaism and the Charybdis of contemporary slang. Tone and atmosphere are as much parts of poetry as image and metre, and the injection of modish slang into a poet who lived at the time of the First World War is as fatal to any authenticity as the superimposition of a senselessly archaic literariness. At times an invisible discreetness appears the most one can hope to achieve. One must admit, too, that if all poems are untranslatable, some are more untranslatable than others. No one is ever going to translate Blok's *The Twelve* adequately, since there is simply no English equivalent for the raucous Russian slang that gives the poem its atmosphere. With Esenin, much has to be written off: the wry affectionate tone of voice, the subtly judged slanginess—these qualities cannot even be striven after. Granted that translation is an attempt to communicate as many as possible of the original poem's information units, it has to be admitted that a good many of these units have no conceivable equivalent outside the particular semantic system which generated them. Poetry exploits the gaps in language and the gaps often afford the reader the generative tension which so frequently fails to happen in translation.

Geoffrey Thurley
University of Adelaide

CONFESSIONS OF A HOOLIGAN

Already evening. Dew
Glistens in the nettles.
I stand at the roadside
Leaning against a willow.

The great light of the moon
Falls full upon our roof.
I hear a nightingale
Singing somewhere far-off.

I feel good and warm, grand
As the winter stove.
And like big candles stand
The birches of the grove.

And far away, beyond
The river and the town,
A drowsy watchman knocks
His dead stick on the ground.

1910

Night

Silently sleeps the river.
The dark pines hold their peace.
The nightingale does not sing,
Or the corncrake screech.

Night. Silence enfolds.
Only the brook murmurs,
And the brilliant moon turns
Everything to silver.

Silver the river,
And the rivulets.
Silver the grass
Of the fertile steppes.

Night. Silence enfolds.
All sleeps in Nature
And the brilliant moon
Turns everything to silver.

1911

The Birch Tree

White birch tree
At my window,
Decked in a dress
Of silver snow.

Its downy branches
Spread thick-fringed
Snowy bunches
Of white selvage.

Still stands the birch
In dream attired;
And the snowflakes burn
In a golden fire

Till lazy sunrise
Circling round
With silver powder
Dusts the boughs.

1913

Riding; so quiet I can hear
The hoofbeats falling on the snow.
Only the grey crows career
Noisily across the meadow.

Under an unseen wizard's spell,
The woods dream fairytale sleep.
A pine I watch is tied up well
Like a white handkerchief.

And stooping like a crippled crone
Bent over her stick half way
Perched on the topmost point, alone,
A woodpecker pecks away.

I gallop on, in endless space.
Snow falls, and softly knits its shawl.
Ahead the highway bounds apace
As ribbon unrolls from a ball.

1914

After the snow, the piles of drying clay.
The foothills sprout a mushroom mass.
The wind is dancing about the plain,
Like an affectionate red ass.

Of pine and willow smells the air;
Heaven slumbers now, and now sighs.
In the pulpit of the forest there
A sparrow reads his Psaltery.

Last year's leaves litter the ravine
Beneath the shrubs, a copper mass,
And a man in a smock of sunshine
Rides by on the russet ass.

Softer than flax is His hair,
But clouded his face and manner.
The fir-trees bow before him there,
And greet him with *Hosanna!*

1914

Autumn

Along the bluff the juniper grove is still.
Autumn like a red mare combs her mane.

Along the banks that guard the river
You hear the blue clink of her hoofs.

The monkish wind with cautious tread
Disturbs the leaves along the highway wall

And kisses on the rowan tree
The scarlet ulcers of the unseen Christ.

1914–16

Wake me tomorrow morning early,
long-suffering mother of mine.
I go out beyond the travel-mound
To welcome the long-expected guest.

Today I saw in a thicket
Broad wheel-marks in the ground.
The wind pulls under the cloudy vault
His golden shaft.

Bending his moon cap under the bush,
tomorrow at dawn he flies.
And playfully his mare will shake
her red tail over the plain.

Wake me tomorrow morning early,
Light a lamp in the best room.
For soon they say I shall become
A famous Russian poet.

I'll sing about you, and our guest,
our stove, our cock, and our home.
And over my poems will flow
The milk of your russet cows.

1917

Beyond the hills, beyond the yellow valleys,
The village footpath stretches, unmetalled;
I see the forest in the evening's blaze,
The fences twined with nettles.

There from morning the sands of the sky
Turned blue above the church's towers.
Damp breezes off the lakes fly,
Ringing through the roadside flowers.

Not for the spring song over the plains
Are the green spaces dear to me still.
I love with the love of the yearning cranes
The monastery on the hill.

At evening when the sky turns misty,
And sunset hangs the bridge above,
At this hour, you go my wretched country
And bow to the Cross and to love.

Gentle souls of that cloistered place,
Avidly hearing the Angelus toll,
Before the Saviour's gentle face,
Pray for my shipwrecked soul.

1916

Country of rains
and foul weather; nomadic silence;
like a white loaf hung
in the zenith, your
moon is broken.

Beyond the ploughland grows
the raspberry-coloured goosefoot.
A ripe star glows
golden on the boughs
of cloud, like a fruit.

Again along the highroad,
your sorrow notwithstanding,
I breathe with bliss the smell
of the summer corn
along the water turning blue.

The marsh mist smokes and thickens.
But in the felt, melodious dark
your hills are satisfied,
in animal dumbness replete.

1917

Not for nothing have the winds
and thunder roared and raved.
Some secret being slaked
my eyes with peaceful light.

With something of a springtime
tenderness, I ceased to grieve
into the azure haze
of earth's unearthly beautiful
enigma.

The silent galaxies do not oppress me now,
nor the starry terror appall me:
for I have learned to love
the world and eternity as I have loved
the hearth of home.

Everything in them is blessed
and holy, all horrors are sublime.
The scarlet poppy of sunset slowly
stains the glass lake. Despite

my will, resistlessly, the image
in the sea of corn is torn
from the tongue: the calving sky
licks the red calf just born.

1917

Ploughed fields, ploughed fields, ploughed fields!
Provincial ennui . . .
Upon my heart hang yesterdays
But Russia shines within.

Beneath the hoofs like little birds
The miles go whistling by.
And handfuls of rain the sun hurls
Sparkling over me.

O country of terrible floods,
Of gentle springtime strength.
Dawn and starlight schooled, my childhood
Unwound here its length.

Here it was I read and pondered
The Bible of the wind.
And here with me Isaiah tended
The herds of golden kine.

1917–18

1.

My golden earth! You bright
Cathedral of Autumn!
A flock of geese takes flight
For the clouds, calling.

Transfigured souls! A horde
Innumerable, that flies
From lakes of sleep towards
Gardens of Paradise.

In front a swan is flying,
Its eyes sad as a grove.
—You, in the sky crying,
My Russia on the move.

Fly on, fly on without fear.
All things have bourne and term.
The wind crowds into song
And the song vanishes in time.

2.

The sky is like a bell,
The moon a tongue's lick.
My mother's my country,
And I a Bolshevik.

For universal
Fraternity
I celebrate in song
Your death, my country.

Powerful and strong,
I take the moon and beat
Heaven's azure gong
At your defeat.

Brothers of all races,
My song is made for you.
Enveloped in mist
I hear the shining hews.

3.

And here is the dove, borne
Aloft in the wind's hands.
It smokes with a new dawn,
My rustic Jordan land.

I praise you, dove, who weld
The vault with stars of ice.
My hands in prayer are held
To ancestral paradise.

I see you, grassy plains,
Swarming with chestnut herds,
And there Saint Andrew plays
His flute among the pollards.

On the edge of the village,
A maiden-mother, sick
And angry with Knowledge,
Beats an ass with a stick.

4.

Ah, brothers, brothers! Men!
Will we not all some day
Live in that blessed region
Where trails the Milky Way?

Do not regret the dead,
The dying; better far
The blooming lilies there,
Than our fresh pastures here.

Love's guardian's a sinner.
Time's cradled by sorrow,
Not content. Today's winner
's a beggar tomorrow.

5.

O new, new, new! Day
Cut from the swarm of days!
Youth with the head of a sun,
Come, sit by me at the fence.

And let me comb your hair
With the moon's fine comb,
For we have learned to greet
The stranger with this custom.

Maurice's ancient shade,
Cousin of our hills,
Abraham visits our fields
With a shower of rain.

Come down to me on the wing,
In peace perch on my arm.
I will light a blue star
As a candle for you.

And I will pray to you,
And praise your Jordan land.
And here is the dove, borne
Aloft in the wind's hand.

June, 1918

Mare Ships

1.

If the wolf bays a star
Cloud has consumed the sky.
Ripped-open bowels of mares,
And the crows' black sails glide by.

The azure thrusts no claws
Through the snow's coughing stench.
Gold-coned a garden of skulls
Circles beneath the whinnying storm.

You hear the cheerful knocking?
—Sunset raking the groves.
With chopped-off hands for oars,
You row to the promised land.

Swim higher, higher yet.
From rainbow fly, crow-crake.
Soon will the white tree let
Fall my head's yellow leaf.

2.

Who are you calling, field?
Is this a pleasant dream?
—Blue cavalry, the rye
Outpacing woods and villages.

Not rye but frost leaps the field.
Smashed windows, gaping doors.
Even the sunlight freezes
Like a gelding's stale piss.

My Russia, is this you? Whose bucket
Scours the scum of your snows?
Along the roads the voracious hounds
Of dawn devour the land.

They need not fly 'thither':
Warmer to survive with man.
God tossed the she-wolf a child,
Man ate the she-wolf's cub.

3.

Who's then to sing? O who,
In this mad blush of corpses?
Look: women hatch a third
Eye slowly from the womb.

There! He crawls out, regards
The moon, sees no fleshed bone.
I sang the wondrous guest, it's clear,
In self-derision.

And where are the other
Eleven with their tapers?
If you must marry, poet,
Take a sheep in a byre.

Involve with straw and wool;
Word-wax warm when you sing.
Evil October strews from the brown
Birch-hands its rings.

4.

You beasts, come near, weep out
Your grief in my cupped hands.
Isn't it time the moon
Stopped lapping the sky's clouds?

Bitch-sisters, brother-hounds!
I join you in the human pen.
Needing no ships of mares,
No sails of ravens.

If from the broken walls
Hunger seize me by the hair,
Half my leg I'll eat myself,
And half toss you to gnaw.

I do not go with man;
Better to starve with you
Than with a loved-one raise the ground,
Stone for a fellow maniac.

5.

Yet I will sing! I'll sing!
Insulting neither goat
Nor hare. If we can mourn a thing,
So can we smile at it.

We all bear the apple of joy.
Close is the blast of the thief.
Autumn's wise gardener
Will crop my head's yellow leaf.

Only one path to dusk garden.
October wind bullies the grove.
To know all things, and take nothing,
A poet came into the world.

He came to kiss the cows,
Heart-hear the oaten crunch.
Cut deeper, sickle-poems.
Strew bird-cherry, bush of the sun!

1919

I am the last poet of the village,
A humble wooden bridge of song.
I stand before the Requiem Mass
Of incense-bearing birch-trees long.

A candle with a golden flame
Burns in its flesh of wax. And soon
My midnight hour will be proclaimed
On the wooden clock of the moon.

And soon the iron guest appears
On the path of the pale blue plains,
Its swift black hands devouring ears
Of the dawn-saturated grain.

Alien mechanic palms, these songs
Are not meant for you.
The faithful horses' ears still mourn
To the old master still true.

The wind will drink their whinnying,
Leading the dance of death. And soon
My midnight hour will hoarsely ring
On the wooden clock of the moon.

1920

Hooligan

A shower with its damp brooms scours
The fields of the willows' refuse.
Spit on, O wind, your leaves in showers.
I am a hooligan like you.

I love it when the blue groves heave
As heavy-gaited bullocks
Their stomachs rumbling with leaves
Stain the trunks on their knees.

And here they are, my cows!
Who better than I to sing them?
I see, I see the dark blot out
The footmarks made by passing men.

O Russia, my wooden Russia!
I am your last poet. I fed
The sadness of my brutish poems
On mignonette and mint. So, then,

Midnight, draw up the moon's jug
And ladle the milk of the birches.
It seems as if the graveyard loved
To choke men with its crosses!

Black terror walks the hills and floods
Our garden with the robber's stealth.
Only, I am the thief, by blood
One of the horse-thieves of the steppe.

Ah, who has watched the trees at night
Boiling in wind? I should have been
Out on the blue steppes, lying in wait,
With a great club somewhere unseen.

A bush was my pillow, and song
With its slavery my nurse.
In a tower of feelings I live condemned
To the endless treadmill of verse.

Ah, senseless wind, I mean no wrong.
In peace blow your leaves about.
Spare me the name of poet. In song,
I too am hooligan, and lout.

1920

Not every man can sing,
Not every apple chances
to fall at a stranger's feet.

Herewith the greatest confession
hooligan ever confessed.

I walk unscathed, resolute, my head
like a kerosene lamp on my shoulders.
Deep in this murk it pleases me
To enlighten the leafless autumn of your souls.
It pleases me now the abusive stones
bombard me like broadsides of belching thunder.
I only squeeze the more tightly
the flailing bladder of my hair.

Then it is well I recollect
the dew-pond and the alder's husky whispering,
recall that somewhere I have parents
who scorn every line I write,
who yet love me like flesh and field,
like the shower that loosens the green in spring,
who would avenge with pitchforks
each shout you hurl at me.

Poor, poor peasants!
How ugly you made yourselves
with your fear of God and the swampy recesses.
O, if you could but understand
your son's the finest poet in Russia!
Your hearts did not grow grey for his life
when he paddled barefoot in puddles,
why now then when he wears
a top-hat and silk shirts?

The ardour of the village boy still
burns in him.
He greets from afar each cow
that adorns a butcher's sign.

And meeting coachmen on the square
remembering the manure smell of his homeland fields,
he's ready to carry every horse's tail
like the train of a wedding-dress.

I love my home,
I love so much, so very much.
Gnawed as it is with grief's willow-rust,
the filthy snouts of its hogs are sweet to me;
and the angry jabots' voices in the silent night.
I'm sick with fondness with childhood memories,
I dream of the damps and mists of April nights.
Our maple squats before the bonfire dawn,
Toasting itself on its haunches.
How many eggs I thieved from the rooks'
nests, swaying in its forks.
And is its green tower still the same,
its bark as tough as it was?

And you my favourite
faithful mangy bitch!
blind and shrill with age,
you wander now about the yard,
your tail scrawny between your legs,
confusing the scent of gate and byre.
How sweet the pranks that I remember,
filching a crust of bread from mother,
and nibbling it together, sharing
the last crumb with each other.

I'm still the same.
At heart, I'm still the same. My eyes
light up in my face
like cornflower in the rye.
Strewing a grassy mat of poems,
I should like to say something tender.
Good night.
To all of you, good night.
The dew is tinkling in the gloomy twilight grass.

Blue world, O blue, blue world!
Even to die into this blueness would be no pain.

What if I should seem the cynic,
tying a rear-light to my tail?
Ancient, good, worn-out Pegasus,
Do I need now your gentle canter?
I came like an austere craftsman
to sing and celebrate the rats.
Like August my head fades
its wild hair with wine.

I want to be a yellow sail,
sailing to the land we're heading for.

November, 1920

No, no, no! I do not want at all to die.
Those birds call overhead in vain. I wish
I were a boy again, shaking copper from the aspen grove,
Holding his palms out like slippery white dishes.
Die? Shall the thought lodge in my heart
When I still have my house in Penzensky?
Sad is the sun, sad the moon, sad the poplar
That waves above the window to me.
Groves, streams, steppe, green things all
Are blessed only for the living.
Listen! I scorn the universe itself
If tomorrow I shall not exist.
I want to live, to live, to live,
Unto terror and sickness live!
Even as pickpocket and thug
So I but see the fieldmice tumble in the field for joy,
So I but hear the bullfrog sing in triumph in his well.
My white soul splashes in apple blossom.
In blue fire the wind has blown the eye away.
For God's sake teach me,
Teach me and I will do what you will,
I will do what you will, to ring in the garden of man.

1922

I will not weep, regret or scold.
All things pass, like smoke from the apple wood.
Consumed now by withering's gold,
My youth has passed away for good.

And you shall beat like that no more
O heart, caught in the grip of cold.
Nor will the birch-tree country lure
My bare feet wandering as of old.

Ah, wanderlust, rarely, rarely
You agitate my mouths' flame now.
And oh, my squandered innocence,
The bright eye and the fevered brow!

A miser now with my desires,
O life,—or did I dream of you?
As if through early spring-time fires
On a pink horse I galloped through.

We shall all perish, and the bronze
Fades silently from maple-leaves.
Then let us feel forever blessed,
Just that we chanced to flower, and died.

1922

I shall not try to fool myself:
Care's roosted in my misty heart.
Why am I now a charlatan?
Why am I now a hooligan?

I'm not a crook—I don't steal wood,
Or shoot unhappy prisoners.
I'm only a street Arab, one
Who smiles at everyone he meets.

Naughty Moscow boulevardier!
Every back-street mongrel
Round Tvyersky Street knows well
The sound of my light step.

And every drayhorse shakes its head
When I go by. For I'm a friend
To animals and every line
I write cures the bestial soul.

My top-hat's not for women—
My heart can't live in stupid lust.
It's handier, my sadness quenched,
For ladling oats to hungry mares.

Amongst men I have no true friend,
Acknowledging another realm.
I'm ready to take off my finest tie
To hang about a horse's neck.

Already now I cease to ache.
The horror in my misty heart has cleared.
This is why I'm a charlatan.
This is why I'm a hooligan.

1922

Ancient mysterious world of mine,
You quietened like a wind blown out.
The new road's asphalt fingers twine
The village's soft throat about.

With what blind fear in snow-chaos
The clanging terror rocked and swayed.
Good day to you, black Nemesis!
I come out to meet you half way.

O city in your bitter throes
You called us carrion scum. And now
The fields freeze ox-eyed in despair,
Throttled by telegraph-poles.

Strong muscles has the devil's neck,
And lightly wears the iron path.
And what of that? We have been wrecked
Before now, brought down by the wrath.

May the heart find bitter this hymn
Of the rights of beasts—bitter and long.
For thus they dog the wolf, drive him
Into the beater's vice-like trap.

—He falls, and from the gloomy wood
A trigger's pressed—and then the spring
Swift and sudden—the two-legged foe
Is savaged in his turn by fangs.

Welcome, then, favourite beast! Your hide
Does not yield cheaply to the knife.
I too am hunted on all sides.
Through enemies of steel I walk this life,

Like you, forever vigilant.
And even while their trumpets blow
For victory, my mortal leap
Tastes hostile flesh and blood. And though

I too am fallen to the ground,
And writhe into the snowy cave,
A song of vengeance shall resound
On the other side of the grave.

1922

Yes, it's decided—I have quit
My native fields for good.
No more will soughing poplars lift
Their winged leaves over my head.

The low house leans lower without me.
My old bitch died years ago.
God has condemned me to die
An exile on the streets of Moscow.

And yet I love this city of elms,
Flabby and senile as she is,
A golden drowsy Asia sinks
To rest on shining cupolas.

And when the moon comes out at night,
Shining like—God knows how!—
Hanging my head I set my sights
Through backstreets to a favourite bar.

The filthy den is full of noise.
But through the night till dawn I shout
My poems to the whores
And knock back vodka with the pimps and touts.

My heart beats faster and faster,
I keep on saying, pointlessly,
'I'm fallen, the same as you,
There's no getting back up for me!'

The low house leans lower without me.
My old bitch died years ago.
God has condemned me to die,
An exile on the streets of Moscow.

1922–23

Low house with pale-blue shutters,
I could never forget you.
Too many were the recent years
Extinguished in the recent dusk.

Even today I still dream
Of our paddock, field and grove;
Enclosed by the grey cotton print
Of those poor Northern skies I love.

There's no more pleasure for me there;
I would not plunge into its woods.
And yet I know I have forever
The sadly tender Russian soul.

I used to love the grey cranes borne
Honking into meagre distance,
Because they never saw the corn
Replete in the fields' expanse.

They only saw the birch-trees flower,
The leaf-stripped willows, bowed and dry;
And heard the bandit whistling
From which it were easy to die.

And if I wanted not to love—
Alas, it cannot be unlearned.
My native fields are sweet to me
Beneath the cut-price cotton skies.

And that is why of late the days
No longer young sweep by in years;
Why I could never forget you,
Low house with pale-blue shutters.

1924

The evening knits black brows; horses
Stand in the yard; can it be true
That yesterday my youth was spent,
And I fell out of love with you?

Ah, troika, peace; you're late; so what?
Our lives have passed without a trace.
Maybe tomorrow a hospital cot
Will be my final resting place.

Yet, on the other hand, maybe
I'll walk out, cured for good,
To hear the song of rain and trees
As a healthy man would.

And I will forget the dark powers
That harrowed me and laid me waste.
But you I shall always remember,
Only you, sweet tender face.

And if I fall in love again,
Even with the new love, with her,
I'll talk about you, dear girl,
Dear girl I once called 'dear'.

I'll tell how our life flowed away,
I'll even say there was no past.
And you, my headstrong head, oh say,
What have you led me to at last?

Moscow Hospital, 1924

Don't torture me by being cold.
And don't ask me my age.
Seized with a heavy fit, my soul
Shakes like a yellow skeleton.

There was a time when like a child,
I mused into the smoke, and dreamt
Of being famous, rich, reviled
By none, and loved by all I met.

Oh, yes, I'm rich—rich in excess.
I had a top-hat, now it's gone.
I have a single shirt-front left,
And one smart pair of boots, well-worn.

Nor does reputation linger:
From Moscow like a French gamin
My name is trouble's harbinger,
A rather loud stomach rumbling.

And isn't love a tedious show?
You kiss me and your lips are tin.
My heart is over-ripe, I know,
While yours will never ripen.

This mournful tone is premature.
Yet if I must, I greet despair.
Along the burial mounds the pure
Young goosefoot whispers your gold hair.

I wish I were back there again,
In the young goosefoot's sound,
To dream boy-like in smoke again,
In sweet obscurity to drown.

To dream of what is new and rare,
Incomprehensible to earth and grass,
For which there is no human name,
And words cannot say to the heart.

1923

56

Sad now for me to watch your face—
So ill, so pitying: remember,
Only the copper leaves remain
In our love's sad September.

Other lips bore off your warmth,
Your body's vibrancy—in vain,
As if, more than half-dead, your heart
Drizzled itself away in rain.

Well, what of that! I'm not afraid
Of it. Another joy has come
To me: see, nothing has remained,
Only the damp, the yellow dust.

You know I never saved myself
For the smiling life, quiet and staid.
Little of what has passed is dear,
And many the errors I have made.

Ah, life—amusing dissonance!
So it has been, will always be.
Like a graveyard the garden's sown
With the clean bones of the birch-trees.

See, we two have run to seed.
Exhausted, like the garden's guests;
If winter has no flowers, what need
For us to sadden or regret?

1923

No, never have I felt so tired.
Into this grey frost and mire
The skies of Ryazan came before me,
And my good-for-nothing life.

I have been loved by many women,
And more than one loved in return.
Was it for this the dark power
Schooled me in the ways of wine?

O endless nights of drunkenness!
And in debauch the old despair!
Was it for this the eyes devour
As a maggot devours a blue leaf?

Unfaithfulness no longer hurts,
The easy conquest brings no pleasure.
And the gold hay of that hair
Turns, slowly, into a grey flower.

Turns into ash and water,
When the autumn mud oozes black,
I do not regret you, bygone years,
I want to bring nothing back.

I'm so tired of this pointless pain;
A strange smile on my face
I love to bear, in a light frame,
The calm light and the dead man's peace.

It isn't even tedious now
To drag myself from bar to bar.
Just as in a concrete jacket
Man has padlocked Nature,

So, the wild fire dies within me, now,
Dictated by the self-same laws.
Yet still respectfully I bow
To those home fields I used to love.

And to that country where I grew
Beneath the maples, and played on the yellow grass,
I send a greeting to the crows
And sparrows and night-sobbing owls.

Into the distances of Spring I call—
'Into the trembling sky,
Dear birds, broadcast the news:
My scandalling is done.
And let the wind begin
Beneath the sun to tan the rye.'

1923

Only one final trick remains—
To stick my fingers in my mouth,
And whistle! Now my evil name
—Foul-mouthed brawler—has got about.

Ah, how farcical this waste was!
Farcical waste in life's not new.
Ashamed I once believed in God,
I'm bitter I no longer do.

Ah, you endless golden distance!
All living matter burns away.
I only played the hooligan
To burn with an intenser flame.

The poet's gift is luxury.
Despair is his native mode.
Here on earth I wished to marry
The white rose and the black toad.

Rosy ambitions of those days—
If only they had not come true!
If devils roosted in my soul
It means that angels lived there too.

What happy turmoils come of this;
Setting out for the other land,
At the last moment I would ask
Of those who chanced to be at hand,

Just that, for all my grevious sins,
And all my disbelief in grace,
They lay me in a Russian shirt
To die beneath an Ikon's face.

1923

This present sadness is not eased
By the light laugh of bygone days.
My white lime-tree has gone to seed,
And sung is my dawn of nightingales.

Then everything around seemed young
To me, and passions thronged my heart;
Now even the tender word is wrung
Like bitter fruitage from my lips.

Familiar sights of space no more
Are beautiful under the moon.
Ravines and hillsides, fields of hemp,
All sadden Russia's endlessness.

Unhealthy, ailing, flat, this drear
Grey waterlogged terrain to me
Is second nature, and so near
My tears spring all too easily.

Small houses, ricketty and frail;
Sheep bleat, and far off in the wind
A horse shakes its abundant tail
Mirrored out in water grey and unkind.

For this we call this land our mother,
All these things we hymn and praise;
Weep for her in the foulest weather,
Await the smiles of better days.

Wherefore this sadness is not eased
With laughter as when we were young.
My white lime-tree has gone to seed,
My dawn of nightingales is sung.

June, 1924

To Pushkin

Thinking of that great gift,
His who is Russia's Fate,
I stand on Tvyersky Street,
Stand and commune with myself.

Blonde, almost albino,
Swathed in a mist of myths,
Pushkin you were a rake
As I a hooligan.

But those sweet escapades
Have not dimmed your image.
Enwrought in bronze glory
You throw back your proud head.

I stand as at a Mass
And answer that I would die
Of happiness being thought
Worthy of such a fate.

But doomed to persecution
I must sing longer yet
That my song of the steppe
Ring out in sounding bronze.

1924

Ah, old one, are you still alive?
I am, and I give you welcome.
May this unearthly evening light
Flood down on the old home.

They tell me you hide your alarm,
But that I soon made you despair.
You often go out on the road
In a dress old-fashioned and threadbare.

In the blue dusk mist I see you,
Always the same, to the life,
As if in a pub brawl some man
Thrust in my heart a Finnish knife.

Calm yourself, old one, it's nothing,
An oppressive nightmare, no more.
I am not yet so bitter a drunk
As, without seeing you, to die.

I'm still as tender as before,
Dream only of the time when I
Forced by rebellious despair
Shall come back to our little house.

I'll come back when the garden spreads
Its branches wide in spring again.
I'll only beg you not to rouse
Me with the cock, as once you did.

Why rouse the spent dream? or disturb
What failed to materialize?
Too much in this life have I learned
Too early waste and weariness.

And don't teach me to pray. What need?
There is no going back to then.
You are my only help and comfort,
You are my one unearthly light.

And so, old girl, forget your fears.
And don't be so quick to despair.
Be seen less often on the road
In a dress old-fashioned and threadbare.

1924

Stanzas

I know a lot
about my talent.
Poetry—there isn't much to it.
More than anything though
it was love for the place
I was born in wearied,
tortured, burned me out . . .

Turn out a rhyme—
for Christ's sake anyone can do it—
girls, the stars, the moon.
But another emotion altogether
gnaws at my heart,
different dreams
oppress my skull.

I want to be citizen
and bard,
a pride and example,
a real son,
not a bastard
to the great Soviet state.

For a long time I fled Moscow.
I have no art
in handling the police:
after every drunken scandal
they held me
in a cell.

I thank those good citizens for their friendship.
But really
to sleep on a hard bench
and in a drunken voice
to read some poem
about the caging
of an unhappy canary—
that's no fun.

I'm not a canary—
I'm a poet!
I'm not what Demyan writes
even if I am sometimes drunk
—in return for that, my eyes shine
with the light of wild recoveries.

I see everything
and understand clearly
this new era is
not a pound of raisins to you,
that the name of Lenin
resounds like the wind

about the world,
generating thoughts
like the sails of a windmill.

Turn, turn, dear sails!
A benefit is promised you.
I am a nephew to you—
you are my uncles.
Come on, Esenin,
let's sit quietly at our Marx,
guessing at the wisdom
of his boring lines.

The days like rivulets
run into the misty river.
The cities flash by
like letters across paper.
Not long ago it was Moscow,
today I'm in Baku.
Tchagin dedicates
an industrial poem to us.

'Look', he says, 'aren't
these gushers of oil, fountains
of oil, better than churches—
We've had enough mystic mist.
Poet, sing what
is living and mighty!'

There is oil on the water
like a Persian blanket.
Evening has spread a veil
of stars across the sky.
Yet I am ready
with a pure heart to swear
that street lighting in Baku
is better than the stars.

I'm possessed by thoughts
of industrial power.
I hear the voice of human strength.
We've had enough
of these celestial lights—
it's easier for us
to build this on earth.

And looking myself straight
in the eye, I say:
'Our time has come.

Come on, Esenin,
let's sit quietly at our Marx
and guess
at the depth of his boring lines.'

1924

The storm has passed. And few of us survive.
At the roll-call of friends are many absentees.
Once more I go back to the orphaned land
I have not visited these past eight years.

Who is there I can call? With whom to share
The sad joy of having remained alive?
Even the windmill here, that wooden bird
With one stiff wing, stands eyes shut-tight.

Nobody knows me here, and those who might
Remember me forgot me long ago.
And where my father's cottage used to stand
Lie ashes covered by the roadside dust.

Life surges on. Around me throng
Faces of young and old, yet not one
To raise my hat to, nor yet one
Whose eyes afford me sanctuary.

A host of ideas surges through my brain.—
What is one's 'motherland'?
And is all this a dream?
For almost all these people here I am a gloomy pilgrim
Out of God knows what distant parts.

I!—A native of this village
Whose only chance of being known
Is that here a peasant woman spawned
An infamous Russian poet.

But reason's voice speaks to my heart—
'Think! Why should you be offended?
This after all is but a new
Generation's light burning in the cottages.

Already you've begun to fade.
Other young men sing other songs,
Which by your leave may be more interesting,
Being sired not by the village, but the world.'

Ah, home, my home, how funny I've become—
A dry flush flies to my sunken cheeks,
My native speech lies awkward on my tongue,
I am a stranger in my own country.

And this is what I see:
Peasants in their Sunday best gathering
At their Soviet as they used to at Church,
With awkward unwashed speeches to debate their 'land'.

Already evening and the sunset sprays
Grey fields with watery gold.
The poplars stick their feet along the ditch
Like heifers poking through a gate.

A lame Red Army veteran with a sleepy face
Wrinkles his forehead to remember, with vast
Importance tells of Budionny, and of how
The Reds won through at Perekop at last.

'Well, then, you see, we got him—once, again—
A bourgeois unit we beat in the Crimea . . .'
And the maples wrinkle long ear-like boughs,
And the old women groan into the silent dusk.

Young Communist peasants career down the hill,
Fervently pounding to the accordion,
Singing Demian Bedny's agit-prop,
They deafen the valley with their happy shouts.

What a country! What perverse whim made me
Proclaim myself in verse the people's friend?
My poetry is no longer needed here.
Yes, and perhaps I am superfluous too.

Well, then, forgive me, native shelter.
I am content as I served you well.
So let them not sing me today—
I sang when my country was sick.

I welcome everything, accept
Everything, as it is, ready
To follow to the end the beaten track.
I yield my whole heart up to October and May.
Only my gentle lyre I still hold back.

Her I will not yield up into strange hands,
Not to my mother, my friend, or my wife.
Only to me does she entrust her sounds,
Only to me she sings her gentle song.

Then flourish, young people! Be strong in body.
You have another life, a different song.
I journey alone towards an unknown region,
My rebel soul forever pacified.
But in that age
when enmity of nations is subdued,
When pain and the lie have vanished for good,
then will I sing with all my poet's being
Of that sixth portion of the earth
called simply, Russia.

1924

Letter to my Wife

You remember
of course; you remember
Everything,—how I stood
Close to the wall, and you
walked about excitedly
and threw something
sharp in my face.

You said, it was time
for us to part, my crazy life
had worn you out,
it was time you took things in hand;
as for me, my lot
was to roll on,
downwards.

Darling,
you never loved me.
You didn't see that I was like a horse
dripping with lather, driven
through the human hordes
spurred by a ruthless rider.
You did not see
That I am in dense smoke,
And the shattering of events
That torture me because I do not understand
Where this century of events is taking us.

Face jammed to face,
the face we do not see.
Much is revealed with distance.
When the calm ocean surface boils
The ship falls on rough times.

The earth is a ship
And someone, suddenly,
For the sake of a new life, a new glory,
Seizes the tiller, and drives her
Hard into the thick of storm and tempest.

Now, which of us, standing up on deck,
did not fall down, blench, and curse?
Few are the seasoned souls
Who stay fast in the turmoil.
Then it was that I,
In the wild din, but ripe for work,
Went down into the hold,
Out of the stench of human vomit.

This hold was the Russian bar.
And there I bent over a pint glass
So that, suffering over no one,
I should destroy myself in the drunken fumes.

Darling,
I tortured you.
I saw despair
in your tired eyes
as I squandered myself haphazardly
before your eyes in stupid scandal.
But you did not see
that I lived in thick smoke,
and the shattering blast of things
which torture me because I do not understand
where this century is leading us.

Now years have passed.
I am in a different age.
I think and feel in different ways.

I raise this festive glass and say:
praise and glory to the helmsman!

Today I'm in the grip
of tender feelings.
I remember your sad fatigue
now I will try
to communicate to you
what I was
and what I have become.

Darling, I find it nice to say
I escaped a steep fall,
now I am the most violent
of the Soviets' fellow-travellers.

I am not now
the man I was.
I would not torture you now
as once I did.
In the name of liberty
and glorious work
I'm ready to go to La Mancha.

Forgive me.
I know you are not that—
you live
with an earnest intelligent man.
You do not need our help,
nor do you need me,
not one particle of me.

Then live your life
as your star leads you
under a vault of shadow restored.
Greetings,
remembering you forever,
your
                    Sergei.

1924

I visit again the places of my childhood,
that village
where I grew up,
where a belfry without a cross
now threw up its birch-wood watch-tower.

How much had changed here,
in their wretched, ugly lives.
How many new discoveries
followed hot upon my footsteps.

I could not pick out
our old family home.
No tell-tale maple waved at the window,
and my mother no longer sat in the porch
feeding chicks with mealy bran.

She must be old,
yes, old.
And I looked round the neighbourhood in grief.
How unfamiliar it had become to me!
Only the white mountain was the same,
and the tall
grey rock on the mountain.

And here was the graveyard,
with the crosses crooked,
as if the dead had frozen
gesticulating in vicious hand to hand fight.

Along the path,
came an old man, sweeping the dust with a broom.
'O Stranger!
Tell me, old fellow,
where's Tatyana Esenin's house?'

'Tatyana? . . .
Over there, behind that hut.

And what are you to her?
Relative?
Can it be—not, not her lost son?'

'Yes, I'm her son.
But what's the matter, dad?
Tell me
why are you so offended?'

'Ah, surely, son, you
recognize your grandfather?'

'Ah, grandad, is it you?'

And the sad talk overflowed the path,
splashing the dusty flowers with warm tears.

'You must be getting on for thirty?
And I'm ninety already,
soon in the ground.
You should have come back long ago,'
he said, all the while wrinkling his brow.
'Yes . . . Time!
You're not a Communist?'
'No!'
'Your sisters are Young Communists.
Nasty business. As well cut your own throat.
Yesterday they took the ikons from the shelves,
the Commissar's taken the cross from the belfry.
Now there's nowhere to pray to God.
I slip off into the woods myself,
and pray to the pines.
Maybe He likes it . . .
Well, well, come along home
and see for yourself.'

And we go along between the fields,
I smile at the woods and ploughed land,
And the old man looks at the belfry in despair.

'I'm well, mother, very well.'
And again I wipe my eyes,

and indeed a cow might weep to see
their squalid little nook.
Lenin adorns a calendar on the wall.
This life belongs
to my sisters, not to me.
But still I'm ready to go down on my knees
to see you again, my beloved country.

The neighbours come round,
a woman with a child.
Already no one recognizes me.
Except our old bitch meets me at the gate,
yelping madly, as in Byron.
And sweet land, this is not you,
this is not you.
And I of course am something different.
The more my mother saddens and despairs,
the more gaily my sisters laugh.
Lenin of course is no ikon to me—
I know the world too well by half.
I love my family, and this is why
I still sit down and with an inclination
of the head, bid my sister
have her say.
And she lays on, opening
a fat *Das Kapital*, like a Bible,
of Marx and Engels.
I of course have no wise read
these estimable gentlemen.

And now it's funny to me
how that bright girl
turned my whole world upside down.

. . .

And our old bitch meets me at the gate,
yelping madly as in Byron.

1924

The Rowan Tree Fire

The golden grove has whispered its last
Happy birchen syllables: all's said.
And now the mournful cranes fly past,
No longer lamenting their dead.

Why should they? We are but passers through,
We pass by, call, then take our leave.
The broad moon on its pale blue pool,
The field of hemp, these only grieve.

I stand alone on this bare plain,
The wind-borne cranes fly farther yet;
I think of happy boyhood days,
Yet nothing in my past regret—

Neither the years of futile waste,
Nor my soul's high lilac-time.
That rowan bonfire burning there
Succeeds in keeping no one warm.

The rowan berries do not burn,
The grass does not yellow and die.
As silently as in their turn
The trees shed leaves, I shed these lines.

And if time with his sweeping wind
Rake all up in a useless pile,
Say this at least, the golden grove
Lisped out its last in lovely style.

1924

Now little by little we depart
For that far land of peace and grace.
And I perhaps must soon collect
My perishable chattels and set out.

Sweet birch groves, and you, earth,
And you, sands of the plain! I lack the strength
To hide my dread
Before this horde of parting souls.

I have loved too much on earth
The things the soul owns in the flesh.
Peace to the pines that, spreading their boughs,
Admire themselves in pink waters.

I have thought much in silence.
Sung many songs about myself.
And I rejoice that I have lived
And in this dark world drawn my breath.

I rejoice that I have kissed women,
Walked among flowers, and lounged on grass,
That I have never beaten about the head
Those dumb beasts that are our lower brothers.

I know the groves don't flourish there,
Nor does rye tinkle its swan-like neck.
Wherefore I always feel this dread
To see this horde of souls departing.

I know that in that land will be
No cornfields gleaming gold in haze.
Wherefore those men are dear to me,
Who live with me on earth.

1924

78

Letter from my Mother

What's left now
to think about?
What's now
to write about?
Before me on
the gloomy table
lies open
a letter from my mother.

'Come to us, darling,'
she writes,
'for the Christmas
holidays.
Buy me a shawl,
trousers for Dad.
So many things
we're short of.

I don't like it,
you being a poet,
you've got such
a shocking name.
Much better you'd
followed the plough
in the field from a lad.

I'm old now,
and sick;
if only you'd
been here at home,
I'd have
a daughter,
and a grandson at my knee.

But you've scattered
children about the world,
given your wife away
to another man;
you have no family or friend,

you're deep in pub
water with no moorings.

My darling son,
what's wrong with you?
You used to be so sweet,
so unassuming,
everyone used to say,
how happy he is,
Sergei Esenin.

Well, our hopes in you
have come to nothing.
And it's all the more
galling and sick to me
that your father
hoped you'd get
more money for your poetry.

Whatever you got,
you never sent it home
to us.
That's why
words fade so bitterly,—
I know
from your experience—
people don't give poets money.

I don't like it,
your being a poet,
you've got such
a shocking name.
Much better you'd
followed the plough
in the field from a lad.

Everything's dreary now.
We live in the dark.
We have no horse.
If you were here at home,
it would be all right—
with your brain

you'd get to be president
of the local soviet.

Then we'd be jolly,
no one'd drag at us,
and you wouldn't have
this useless tiredness.
I'd make your wife spin,
and you would look after us
in our old age,
like a son should.'

       .   .   .

I crumple the letter,
plunged into horror.
Is there no way clear
of this predestined path?
But everything I think
I'll tell now
in the letter I answer with.

1924

The Reply

Dear old lady,
live on as you are living.
Tenderly in my heart I hold
your love, your memory.
But only you, perhaps,
can understand nothing
of my life, my purposes.

You have winter now,
and on these moonlit nights,
I know, you are not alone
in thinking
that someone is swaying
the cherry tree
and spreads snow
at the window.

Flesh of my flesh!
Well, how can you sleep
in a blizzard?
It roars so woebegone,
so long drawn out
in the chimney.
You'd like to go to sleep,
but you see
not a pillow, but a narrow grave,
in which you are being buried.

Like a thousand
snuffling demons
it screams and wails—
riff-raff blizzard!
and the snow falls
like flocks of birds,
and there is neither wife
nor friend beyond the grave.

I love the spring,
most of all,
I love the ravine,
with the striving brook,
where every splinter's
like a ship—
such spaciousness
the eye cannot fathom.

But the Spring I love
I call
the great Revolution.
Only for her
do I suffer and scandalize,
only her do I wait for,
and invoke.

But this filth—
this cold cold planet!
Why shouldn't it burn,
burn at the Lenin sun!
This is why
I started my rowdying,
started drinking, acting up,
with the sick soul of a poet.

But the time will come,
sweet old lady,
the longed for hour will strike!
we did not take up arms
for nothing,
this one the machine-gun,
this one the pen.

Forget about money, then,
forget everything.
What disaster!?
Is this you? Is it?
You see, I'm not a cow,
a horse, a sheep

to be led
out of its stall.

I will leave myself
when the hour comes round,
when we must
burn about the planet,
and, returning, then
I'll buy you that shawl,
and buy those things for Dad.

Meanwhile, the storm howls on,
like a thousand
snuffling demons
sings and screams—
riff-raff blizzard!
and the snow falls
like flocks of birds,
and there is neither wife
nor friend beyond the grave.

1924

Spring

The paroxysm has passed.
Sadness is in disgrace.
I welcome life like the first dream.
Yesterday in *Das Kapital* I read
that poets own
their own law.

Now snowstorm
with your devil howl
knock like a naked drowned man—
with my severed head still
am I a cheerful happy comrade.

We do not weep for carrion,
nor would there be need to weep for me
if in this snowy tumult
I could die submissively.

Twit-twit! you tomtits.
Good morning!
Don't be afraid—
I will not harm you.
Perch if you will
on the wattle
according to your bird-law.

A law of revolution obtains—
the relations
between all living things.
If you but share a single meal with man,
you have the right
to sit and lie with him.

Welcome to you,
my poor old maple!
Forgive my insulting you.
Your clothes are tatters
but you shall be dressed anew.

With no invoice, April
doffs her green cap to you,
and silently
enfolds you
in armloads of tender swaddling.

And a girl comes out to you
and feeds you well-water,
so you can fight
with grim October blizzards.

At night
the moon swims out.
The dogs didn't gobble her up—
she was invisible
through the bloody
human brawl.

But the brawl is over.
Look—
with her citrous light
she floods the trees
dressed in new green
with ringing radiance.

Then sing, my breast,
of spring! Rock
with new poems!
Today I will not curse
the cocks on my way
to sleep.

Earth, earth,
you are not steel.

Can steel push up
these shoots?
Enough to hit
the thread,
—and suddenly I understand
Das Kapital.

1925

A dream: black road.
White horse. Stubborn foot.
And on the horse
rides someone dear,
rides someone dear
I do not love.
    Ah, Russian birch,
    narrow pathway.
    only that one
    dear as sleep, her
    hold with your boughs
    like expert hands.
Moonlight. Blue, sleep.
The horse clops well.
Such music light
for that unique
one, she who holds such light,
but not exists.
    A hooligan,
    maudling with rhymes.
    At a mad career
    to keep the heart hot,
    through birchy Russia
    to meet with her,
    my non-beloved.

July, 1925

Goodbye Baku; I won't see you again.
Now grief and fear possess my soul.
The heart beneath my hand is close
And sick; I feel more strongly the simple word, Friend.

Goodbye Baku, and goodbye Turkish blue!
The blood grows cool, powers weaken.
But I will carry to the grave, like happiness,
The Caspian waters and May in Balakhar.

Goodbye Baku! Goodbye, a simple song,
For the last time I embrace my friend.
Would that his head like a golden rose
Beckoned me onward in the lilac smoke.

May, 1924

Falling leaves, falling leaves,
And the wind's moan
Drawn out long and dull.
Who will rejoice my heart?
Who will calm my heart, my friend?

With the burdened centuries
I stare and stare at the moon.
And again the cockerels crow
Into the strange stillness.

Hour before dawn. Blue. Early,
Blessings of falling stars.
You'd guess some wish—
But I don't know what to wish for.

What's to wish for under this life's burden,
This accursed lot and home?
I wish, I wish a beautiful girl
Would pass by under my window
With cornflower eyes for me
And me alone,
And no one else—
One who would soothe my heart and soul
With new words and new feelings.

And welcoming happiness
Under the white moonlight,
I should not melt over songs,
Be too much moved,
And with someone's else's happy youth,
Should not regret my own.

August, 1925

To my sister, Shura

I am just a passer-by on earth,
So wave your happy hand to me.
The autumn moon has such a light
Of mild tranquillity.

For the first time I warm myself
At the moon, glow from the cold.
Again I live, and live in hope
Of love which I have never known.

Our lowland flatness brought this on,
Salted by the whiteness of sand,
And someone's tousled innocence,
And someone's native despair.

I will not hide forever, then,
That love is not a thing apart.
One love together shared brought us
This country of the heart.

Moscow, September 25, 1925

The flowers say goodbye to me,
Bending their heads down low they say
That never again shall I see
My native region and her face.

Well, well, darlings, well, well; well, well.
I saw you and I saw the earth,
And like a new sort of caress
I welcome now the dread of death.

And because I have always seized
All life as it smiled its way past,
So at every moment I say,
That everything comes back at last.

For all's the same: comes someone new,
The pain of the last is still as strong.
The new arrival sings the dear
Deserted girl a better song.

And humming the song in the dark
With her new lover, then, maybe,
As of a flower that won't come back
She'll sometimes think of me.

1925

Snow-bound plain under moonlight.
Savannah-covered country.
Birches through the wood weep white
Mourning whom? Surely not—me?

October 4-5, 1925

Pushkin wrote about Delvig,
drooling out lines about
his skull.
So excellent and so far,
yet still so near,
like an orchard in bloom.

Greetings, my sister,
Greetings! Greetings!
Am I, or am I not, a peasant?
How is granddad nursing along
our cherry-trees now in Ryazan?

Ah, those cherry-trees!
You haven't forgotten them?
And how much trouble father took
to make our lean
and rusty mare
plough up the root-crops!

He needed potatoes,
we the orchard.
They ploughed up the orchard,
yes, ploughed it up!
a damp pillow knows
all about that . . . seven
or eight years back.

I remember the feast,
the bell-swung feast of May.
The bird-cherry was in bloom,
and the lilac, and every birch-tree,
and I was more drunk than the azure day itself.

Birches! Girl-birches!
he only cannot love them,
who even in the luxuriant sapling
cannot divine the root.

94

Sister! My sister!
How few friends one ever really has.
The stamp is on me,
as on everyone . . .
if that tender heart of yours
is tired,
make it forget, and hold its peace.

You know Pushkin was good . . .
And Lermontov
as good.
But I am sick
and only the pollen
of the lilac-bush
can cure my heart now.

I'm sorry for you.
You'll be left alone,
and I'm ready to take my bow,
even if to a duel.
'Blessed is the man who has not drained the cup'
or heard the voice of Pan.

But ah, our orchard,
the orchard . . . in spring
your spoiled kids will walk through it.
Oh, let them only remember
from time to time
that once there lived

strange birds on the earth.

1925

Purple evenings, lunar nights!
Once I was handsome and young.
Resistless, never to return,
Everything flows—farther—past.
The heart cools down, the eye fades.
Purple happiness! Lunar nights!

1925

My Path

My life is heading for the bank.
A one-time villager
I remember what I saw
in the country.
Quietly, my poems,
tell of my life.

A peasant hut,
a smell of pitch and harness,
an old ikon-frame,
the soft light of the lamp.
—How good to have preserved
these childhood sensations.

At the window
is the white fire of the blizzard.
I am nine.
Stove-bed, grandma, cat.
And grandma singing
some sad song
from the steppes,
now and then yawns
and covers her mouth.

The blizzard howled
under the window
as if dead men were waltzing.
Then the Empire
declared war on Japan,
and everyone dreamed
of distant crosses.

I knew nothing then
of Russia's misdeeds.
I did not know why
or for what the war was fought.
The fields of Ryazan

where the peasants mowed
and sowed their grain—
this was my country.

I remember only
that the peasants grumbled,
cursing devil,
God and Tsar.
But only the smiling distance
answered them,
our watery lemon-
coloured dawns.

Then for the first time
I gushed out rhymes.
My head reeled
from the press
of feelings, and I said,
this rash having woken,
I'll bathe myself in words.

You distant years,
now hidden in the mist.
I remember my father
saying sadly,
'An empty business.
But if it draws you,
write of rye-fields,
or better still of mares.'

Then in my brain,
with a close inclination to the Muse,
trickled the thought
of being rich,
and famous, of having
a monument stand to me in Ryazan.

Fifteen years old,
I fell in love,
and sweetly dreamed

—only I retire—
that reaching manhood
I would wed
this paragon of girls.

Years flowed by.
Time changes faces,
a different light
falls on them.
The village dreamer
in the capital became
a first-class poet.

And falling sick
from writer's ennui,
I went off wandering
different countries,
sceptical of meetings,
careless of partings,
taking the whole world for a fraud.

And then I knew
what Russia was,
I knew too
what was glory,
and why it was
despair had come
into my heart
like bitter poison.

What the devil!
I, a poet.
There's enough trash without me.
Let me die,
only—
no;
no monument in Ryazan.

Russia, the Kingdom,
despair,
a condescending upper-class.

Well, and what of that?
Accept, then, Moscow, a
reckless hooligan.

Let's see—
who welcomes whom?
Watch, while on my poems
a Ryazan mare
stampedes
through the glossy salon rabble.

You don't like this?
Well, you're right,
accustomed to Lorrigan and roses.
But this grain
you're burning—
you see, we too . . .
manure . . .

Still more years passed.
Years in which things happened,
things that can't be said
in words:
in place of the Tsar
appeared the worker army,
with most enormous strength.

Tired of idling
in foreign parts
I came back home.
Green-leaning,
in its white petticoat,
the birch-tree stands over the pond.

Still there, that birch.
Marvellous—but breasts,
such breasts
you will not find on women.
From sun-sprayed fields
people pass me with carts
of rye.

They don't recognise me.
To them, I'm a passing stranger.
But here comes my mother,
not looking up.
I feel along the length
of my spine a shock
of inexpressible emotion.

Surely she—
surely she recognises me?
Well, so be it.
let me pass by.
She's bitterness enough
without me.
That mouth is not set hard
in suffering for nothing.

In the evening,
pulling my hat down low
so's not to show
the cold of my eyes,
I go out to watch the
endless steppe,
and hear the tinkling brook.

Well, so what?
My youth has gone.
Time now to occupy myself
so that
this delinquent soul of mine
sing grown-up songs.
And may another village life
fill me with new strength,
as once a native Russian mare
pulled me to glory.

1925

Ah friend, my friend,
how sick I am. Nor do I know
whence came this sickness.
Either the wind whistles
over the desolate unpeopled field,
or like a September copse
alcohol assaults my brain.

My head waves my ears
like a bird its wings.
Unendurably it looms on my neck
when I walk.
The black
black
black man
sits by me on the bed all night
won't let me sleep.

This black man
runs his fingers down a vile book,
and, twanging over me
like a sleepy monk
indicts the life
of some drunken wretch,
filling my heart with longing and despair.
A black man
oh a black black man.

'Listen, listen,—
he mutters to me—
'the book is full of beautiful
plans and resolutions.
This fellow lived
his life in a land
of the most repulsive
thieves and charlatans.

And in that land the December snow
is pure as the very devil,

and the snowstorms drive
merry spinning-wheels.
This man was a chancer,
though of the highest
and best quality.
Oh he was elegant,
—and a poet at that—
albeit of a slight
but penetrating gift,
he called some woman
—forty or so—his
'filthy whore', his
'beloved'.

Happiness—he said
is quickness of hand and mind.
Slow fools are always
known for unhappy.
Heartaches, we know,
derive
from broken lying gestures
and into thunder and tempest,
and the world's coldheartedness
at times of heavy loss,
and when you are sad
it seems laughably simple—
the best of life is Art.

'Black man!
This is no laughing matter.
You do not live as
deep-sea diver.
What's the life
of a scandalous poet to me?
Please read the tale
of someone else.'

The black man
Looks me straight in the eye
and his eyes screen
vomit-blue—as though
he wanted to tell me

I'm a thief and rogue
who'd robbed a man
openly without shame.

Ah friend, my friend,
how sick I am. Nor do I know
whence came this sickness.
Either the wind whistles
over the desolate unpeopled field
Or like a September copse
alcohol assaults my brain.
The night is freezing.
Still peace at the crossroads
I am alone at the window
expecting neither visitor nor friend.
The whole plain is covered
with soft quick-lime,
and the trees like riders
in our garden conspire.

Somewhere a night-bird
ill-omened is sobbing.
The wooden riders
scatter hoofbeats.
And again the black man
is sitting in my chair,
lifts his top-hat
and, casual, takes off his cape.

'Listen, listen,'
he cries, eyes on my face,
all the time leaning closer.
'I never knew one
of these rogues
stupidly, pointlessly,
suffer insomnia.

Well, I could be wrong.
There is a moon tonight.
What more is needful
in your drunken world than sleep?
Perhaps She will come,

with her fat thighs,
in secret, and you read
your languid carrion
verse to her.

Ah, how I love these poets!
A holy race!
I always find in them
a story known to my heart.
Such as a long-haired monster
sweating sexual lassitude
breathes to a pimply student.

I don't know, don't remember,
in some village,
Kaluga perhaps, or
maybe Ryazan,
there lived a boy
of simple peasant stock,
blonde-haired
and angel-eyed.

And he grew up,
grew up into a poet
of slight but
penetrating talent,
and some woman
of forty or so
called his filthy girl,
his loved one.'

'Black man!
An odious guest!
This ill-fame
is old talk of you.'
Enraged, possessed,
I let him have it—
my cane flies
straight across
the bridge of his nose.

.   .   .

The moon has died.
Dawn glimmers in the window.
Ah, you, night,
what have you covered up all night?
I stand top-hatted;
no-one is with me,
I am alone,
and the mirror is broken.

1925

Suicide Note

Goodbye, my friend, goodbye, goodbye.
You are in my heart, as evidence.
Our preordained disseverance
Predicts reunion by and by.

Goodbye; no handshake to endure.
Let's have no sadness-furrowed brow.
There's nothing new in dying now
Though living is no newer.

1925